GREEN BERETS

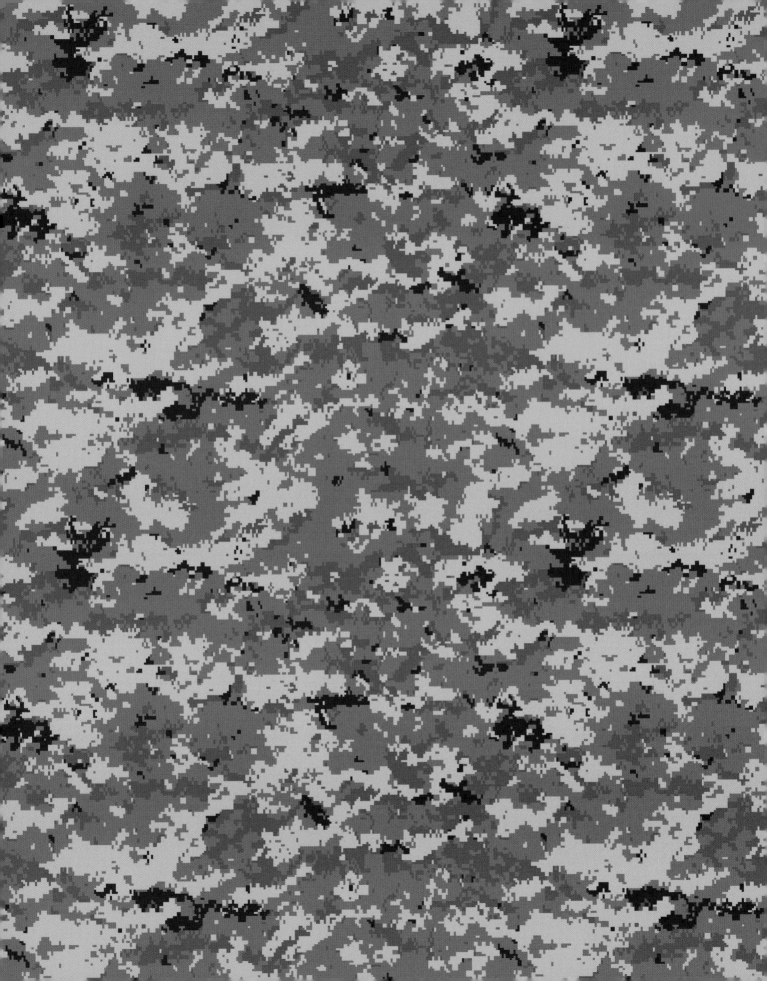

U.S. SPECIAL FORCES

GREEN BERETS

JIM WHITING

CREATIVE EDUCATION

PUBLISHED BY Creative Education

P.O. Box 227, Mankato, Minnesota 56002

Creative Education is an imprint of The Creative Company

www.thecreativecompany.us

DESIGN AND PRODUCTION BY Christine Vanderbeek

ART DIRECTION BY Rita Marshall

PRINTED IN the United States of America

PHOTOGRAPHS BY

Alamy (North Wind Picture Archives, Photos 12, Pictorial Press Ltd,
US Air Force Photo, US Army Photo, ZUMA Press, Inc.), Corbis (AP,
Bettmann, CORBIS, Franco Pagetti/VII, Sunset Boulevard), Getty
Images (Eric Draper/White House), iStockphoto (spxChrome),
Shutterstock (360b, ALMAGAMI, gst, skyearth, zimand), SuperStock
(Exactostock, Stocktrek Images, UNIVERSAL STUDIOS/Album/Album)

LIBRARY OF CONGRESS CATALOGING-IN-PUBLICATION DATA

Whiting, Jim.

Green Berets / Jim Whiting.

p. cm. — (U.S. Special Forces)

Includes bibliographical references and index.

Summary: A chronological account of the American military special
forces unit known as the Green Berets, including key details about
important figures, landmark missions, and controversies.

ISBN 978-1-60818-463-7

1. United States. Army. Special Forces—Juvenile literature. I. Title.

UA34.S64W45 2014

356'.160973—dc23   2013036172

CCSS: RI.5.1, 2, 3, 8; RH.6-8.4, 5, 6, 8

FIRST EDITION

9 8 7 6 5 4 3 2 1

U.S. SPECIAL FORCES

TABLE OF CONTENTS

★ ★ ★

Green Berets practice helicopter insertions at the Special Warfare Center.

FORCE FACTS Special Forces honored president John F. Kennedy by naming its training facility The JFK Special Warfare Center after he was assassinated in November 1963.

INTRODUCTION

CAPTAIN ROGER DONLON AND HIS DETACHMENT OF ARMY Special Forces—more popularly known as Green Berets— arrived in South Vietnam in late May 1964. Along with about 300 South Vietnamese soldiers, Donlon's 12-man team quickly established a small, fortified camp called Nam Dong near the border with Laos. Eventually, more than 200 similar camps would dot the countryside, strategically located to attack enemy supply routes. These attacks were thorns in the side of the Viet Cong (and later North Vietnamese), who worked to eliminate the source of such assaults.

At about 2:25 A.M. on July 6, Nam Dong was attacked by a force of nearly 1,000 Viet Cong who had surrounded the camp and fired mortars, grenades, and automatic weapons. During the savage firefight, Conlon was wounded in his stomach, his shoulder, his leg, and his face. Flying *shrapnel* opened cuts all over his body. Despite his wounds, Donlon continued to direct the camp's defenses as the Green Berets and South Vietnamese fought off wave after wave of attackers. He even administered first aid to some of the other wounded.

American reinforcements finally arrived at about 7:00 A.M. The attackers melted back into the jungle. According to estimates, they had lost more than 200 men. Fifty-five South Vietnamese had also perished, along with two members of Donlon's detachment and an Australian special forces soldier. Later that year, Donlon was awarded the Medal of Honor—the nation's highest military decoration—for his actions. It was the first Medal of Honor awarded during the Vietnam War.

U.S. soldiers had to adapt quickly to Vietnam's wild terrain and jungle conditions.

WEARING THE GREEN

UNITED STATES SPECIAL OPERATIONS FORCES (SOFs) ARE highly trained units in all military branches that perform *unconventional warfare* missions. Many people think of SOFs as men who blow up stuff and seek to destroy their enemies in close quarters combat (CQC), using weapons such as carbines, pistols, and grenades. In the popular imagination, these forces sneak into enemy territory, do their damage, and then get out as fast as they can. Such a scenario was typical of some ancestors of the Green Berets. During the *French and Indian War* (1754–63), for example, a group of Americans known as Rogers' Rangers (named after their leader, Major Robert Rogers) fought on the British side. The operating instructions Rogers gave his men were simple: "Let the enemy come till he's almost close enough to touch, then let him have it and jump out and finish him up with your hatchet."

Besides this tradition of aggressive warfare, Green Berets also draw on a heritage of blending in with their surroundings and attracting *indigenous* support. During the Revolutionary War (1775–83), South Carolina planter Francis Marion was nicknamed the "Swamp Fox" by frustrated British troops who couldn't successfully trail him and his men into their swampy hiding place. Marion was credited with inspiring the locals to resist British plans to split the colonies in half, as well as with

The Swamp Fox's militia rescued prisoners and raided British camps before vanishing again.

attacking supply lines and launching hit-and-run raids that kept his foes off balance.

During World War II (1939–45), the First Special Service Force, a joint American-Canadian commando unit that specialized in mountain and amphibious warfare in Europe, nicknamed themselves "The Devil's Brigade." They often applied stickers emblazoned with their unit patch and the phrase "Das dicke Ende kommt noch" ("The Worst is yet to Come") on the corpses of German soldiers they had killed during silent operations.

Not long after the U.S. entered World War II in December 1941, the Japanese overwhelmed the American and Filipino defenders of the Philippines in a few months. Captain Russell Volckmann disappeared into the jungle rather than surrender. He raised a Filipino army that eventually numbered more than 20,000 men and carried out many raids against the Japanese. By the war's end in 1945, his forces were credited with killing at least 50,000 enemy troops. Volckmann's success depended largely on the willingness of the native Filipino population to conceal and sustain his forces.

Volckmann's experiences convinced him of the value of unconventional warfare. Along with Brigadier General Robert McClure and Colonel Aaron Bank, he pushed for the establishment of special operations forces, even though the American military was focused on atomic weapons and large armies. The result of their efforts was the establishment of the 10th Special Forces Group in 1952. Originally, it consisted of Bank, a *warrant officer*, and seven *enlisted men*. Within a year, the group had expanded to a force of 1,700 troops. Its mission was "to infiltrate by air, sea, or land deep into enemy-controlled territory, and to stay, organize, equip, train, control, and direct the indigenous potential in the conduct of Special Operations Forces."

Army Special Forces was—and still is—very different from Delta Force, a super-secret unit established in the late 1970s

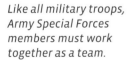

Like all military troops, Army Special Forces members must work together as a team.

FORCE FACTS In the late 1970s, some Green Berets worked in rural areas of the U.S. as part of the Special Proficiency at Rugged Training and Nation Building program to build roads and medical facilities.

that is also part of the U.S. Army. Delta Force specializes in counterterrorism, and its units conduct short-term operations. Although they may occasionally enlist the cooperation of local groups, Delta Force makes little or no effort to train them. Army Special Forces personnel, on the other hand, typically insert themselves into a region and seek out local units, helping train them over extended periods of time. As they have demonstrated many times over, they are also fully capable of taking on their enemies in direct combat.

To strengthen its morale and reflect its sense of distinction, the fledgling organization copied the green beret used by similar units in other countries, even though the headwear was officially banned by the U.S. military establishment. As noted military author Tom Clancy observed, the men "liked the style and swagger it represented. It became a symbol of the Special Forces esprit [liveliness] and professionalism ... and the ban only made SF soldiers wear it more often around their home bases."

After John F. Kennedy became president in 1961, he sided with the Green Berets. Kennedy wanted to fight communist-inspired "wars of national liberation" with small groups rather than massive armies. In October 1961, he visited Fort Bragg, North Carolina, to inspect the elite 82nd Airborne Division. He also wanted to take a look at Special Forces and insisted that they be allowed to wear their trademark headgear. More significantly, Kennedy doubled the size of the Special Forces program, and the Green Berets captured the public imagination with their exploits during the ensuing Vietnam War.

As American involvement in the war continued to escalate, Special Forces grew to

During World War II, Filipino fighters joined with U.S. special forces to resist the Japanese.

13,000 men by 1970. When the war ended five years later, Special Forces began a decline that dropped its numbers to 3,000 by 1980. Despite having fewer personnel, Special Forces expanded its focus to encompass combating the drug trade and communist movements in Central and South America. Though it was hard to make inroads against drug lords, the collapse of the Soviet Union in 1991 basically ended the communist threat.

However, by then a different threat that would engage the Green Berets and other special operations forces had emerged: religiously motivated terrorists who in many cases couldn't be identified with a particular country. One of the key events in this changeover was the capture of the American embassy in Tehran, Iran, in 1979. An operation to free the dozens of hostages the following year ended disastrously, which led to the formation of the U.S. Special Operations Command (USCOM) in 1987. All American special operations forces—including the Green Berets—came under the command of USCOM. The terrorist situation, which had steadily increased in the final years of the 20th century, underwent a dramatic escalation following the 9/11

The small-scale, unconventional style of engagements common in World War II influenced the Green Berets.

attacks. Special Forces found themselves on the leading edge of what became known as the War on Terror.

The basic unit of Special Forces is the 12-man Operational Detachment-Alpha (ODA), or A-team. It is commanded by a captain, with a warrant officer as second-in-command. The remaining 10 men are noncommissioned officers (NCOs), almost always sergeants. Two NCOs are trained in each of four military occupational specialties: weapons, engineering, medical, and communications. The remaining two positions are filled by an intelligence sergeant and an operations sergeant, the latter of whom also serves as the team sergeant. The men are all cross-trained so that they can assume the responsibilities of fellow team members should the need arise.

Six A-teams, along with an Operational Detachment-Bravo (ODB, or B-team), comprise a Special Forces company. The B-team functions as a headquarters group and provides overall command and control for the six A-teams. Three companies of A-teams, a support company (consisting of mechanics, cooks, legal and personnel services, and even a chaplain), and a headquarters group make up a battalion, which is the basic deployment element. Battalions, in turn, are assigned to Special Forces Groups (SFGs). Originally, an SFG consisted of three combat battalions, but as the need for SOFs has increased in recent years, a fourth battalion has been added to each SFG. An SFG also includes a headquarters company—which provides overall administration—and a group support battalion (for logistical, intelligence, medical, and signals assistance).

Training with other special forces parachute jumpers prepares ODAs for cross-unit missions.

FORCE FACTS Part of parachute training involves jumping from high altitudes where oxygen is scarce, so jumpers carry an oxygen supply with them and breathe from it during the descent.

BECOMING A GREEN BERET

U.S. SPECIAL FORCES

UNTIL RECENTLY, ONLY CURRENTLY SERVING MILITARY MEMbers could join Special Forces. However, the combination of *attrition* and the recent expansion of SFGs from three to four battalions opened the door to civilians (between the ages of 20 and 30) to join. Someone who chooses this route must undergo the 30-day Special Operations Preparation Course (SOPC) at Fort Bragg, North Carolina. The primary focus of SOPC is on physical training, with additional emphasis on land navigation. Other candidates—primarily NCOs—are already in the military and wish to take on the greater challenges and increased prestige that comes with joining Special Forces. Officers are almost always captains or first lieutenants who will shortly be promoted. They must have at least three years remaining in their current term of enlistment.

Once they have expressed their interest, potential Green Berets take the 24-day Special Forces Assessment and Selection (SFAS) course. Held at Camp MacKall, North Carolina, it is designed to be as grueling as possible, to push the men to the limits of their mental and physical capacities. They must swim at least 50 meters wearing the same heavy uniforms and boots in which they would go to battle. They also have to navigate obstacle courses, which are not only physically taxing but also serve to identify anyone with a fear of heights or enclosed spaces.

Before they can wear the green beret, candidates endure up to two years of intensive training.

FORCE FACTS Originally, the Green Berets were known as the 10th Special Forces Group in hopes that the Soviet Union and other Cold War enemies would believe there were nine more groups.

The candidates spend most of their time on their feet, either running or marching, and typically wear rucksacks weighing at least 50 pounds (23 kg) in a variety of weather conditions during marches. Often, they aren't told in advance how long the exhausting march will last. "Situation and reaction" exercises test one's ability to think clearly under conditions of extreme fatigue.

Much of what the candidates do in SFAS incorporates team-building exercises such as "caterpillar" pushups, which involve each man placing his boots on the shoulders of the man behind him. Small groups work together in hoisting and controlling a telephone pole, a task that demands coordinated movements. They are also tasked with moving a jeep that has become mired in a pit of soft sand.

As if these tests weren't difficult enough, everyone is intentionally deprived of sleep. So it's not surprising that at least 50 percent of the would-be Green Berets normally wash out before SFAS is even halfway over. Some simply decide that they aren't up to the challenge. Others are bounced by the instructors. And still more are eliminated before the course's end.

The survivors can look forward to the even more intense and demanding Special Forces Qualification course, known simply as the Q course. It lasts for up to a year or, in some cases, even longer. The men learn basic skills such as land navigation, small and large unit tactics, and *infiltration* and *exfiltration* tactics. And every man must master parachuting, *rappelling*, and *fast-roping*.

Another essential aspect of the Q course is the more than three months of Military Occupational Specialty (MOS) training, in which the trainee focuses on his specific role within the team to which he will be assigned. He also spends considerable amounts of time in learning at least one foreign language and gaining insights into the country or countries that speak

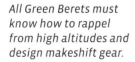

All Green Berets must know how to rappel from high altitudes and design makeshift gear.

that language, helping him to gain the trust and respect of the troops with whom he will eventually be working.

While no one expects to be forced into a situation in which he might be captured, it is necessary to prepare for such a scenario. Every man must take Survival, Evasion, Resistance, and Escape (SERE) training. Some elements of SERE can be especially intense, as "captors" employ a variety of methods to try to break down their "captives."

Of course, much of the training involves weaponry. The men become proficient with a variety of small arms. In common with other SOFs, the basic Special Forces weapon is the M4A1 carbine. It can be equipped with a rail interface system, which allows the user to attach a variety of accessories, such as advanced sighting mechanisms. The most common sidearm is the Beretta M9 handgun. A recent version, the M9A1, includes an accessories rail. For further firepower, the men can choose from among the Remington M870 shotgun, M249 *squad automatic weapon*, a number of sniper rifles, several types of grenade launchers—either standalones or attached to the M4A1—and the Javelin anti-tank missile, which is used when the men encounter enemy armor.

As trainees become more adept at handling their core armament, they also familiarize themselves with dozens of other weapons—many from foreign countries. Chief among these is the Russian-made Kalashnikov. "Of all the rifles available for war today, the Kalashnikov line stands apart as the most abundant and widely used rifle ever made," notes former Marine Corps captain C. J. Chivers. "With its stubby black barrel with a parallel gas tube above, its steep front sight post, and the distinctive banana clip," Chivers continues, "its unmistakable profile has become a constant presence in the news."

U.S. Special Forces use the M4 rifle, a shortened M16 carbine ideal for precision raids.

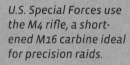

In fact, using Kalashnikovs and other foreign weapons can have several advantages in the field. If the Green Berets are using these weapons and have to abandon them, "native" weapons won't betray the nationality of their users if picked up. This can allow the Berets to remain concealed and help avoid capture. In firefights using "borrowed" weapons, the men can take ammunition from enemies they have killed or disabled. And most weapons have a distinctive sound. Enemy forces that cannot see the action might be deceived into believing that their own soldiers are firing the weapons they hear.

To see how well the trainees have learned their lessons, in one exercise during the latter part of their training, assorted parts from different weapons are thrown into a pile. The men have to assemble each weapon and be ready to use it within a certain time limit.

Once training is complete, the "graduation exercise" still remains. Named Robin Sage, this exercise lasts for 2 weeks and typically encompasses 15 counties and 8,000 square miles

The green berets feature a colored badge representing the soldier's assigned group.

(20,720 sq km) in central North Carolina. Centered on the fictional country of Pineland, Robin Sage involves thousands of local citizens who volunteer for roles ranging from *guerrilla* leaders to ordinary citizens. Other trainees and Special Forces personnel who aren't currently deployed also take part.

As Majors Gregory Parks and Ed Williams note in the magazine *Special Warfare*, "During the scenario, [Q course] students work to assist the government of Pineland, which is facing an *insurgency*. Following a *coup* that deposes the legitimate government, the SF students work with role players to raise and train a guerrilla force that will fight the usurpers and attempt to restore the Pineland government. The unique training area and unconventional-warfare, or UW, training environment allow instructors to stress the SF candidates, assessing their ability to think on their feet and accomplish their team's missions."

Completing Robin Sage may be the final step in a Green Beret's initial training, but there are further courses that the men can take to increase their effectiveness. The Combatant Commanders In-extremis Force (CIF) Company is one example. CIF focuses on counterterrorism operations and includes both the training of foreign tactical units and the carrying out of such missions themselves. First, CIF trainees undergo the eight-week Special Forces Advanced Reconnaissance, Target Analysis, and Exploitation Techniques Course (SFARTAETC). While exact course details are classified, the primary emphasis is on close quarters combat in urban situations.

Another specialty course is mountaineering. Students acquire expertise in such disciplines as tactics in mountainous terrain, guiding inexperienced troops over rocks and similar obstacles, and how to utilize pack animals. Or they can expand their basic scuba skills by taking the Special Forces Combat Diver Qualification Course (SFCDQC), which provides them with skills and expertise in a variety of underwater situations.

Continued language training is also important. Green Berets are expected to be fluent in at least one other language, and many know more than that. In recent years, knowledge of Arabic and Farsi (the language of Iran, Afghanistan, and Middle Eastern and Central Asian countries) has proven critical.

Mountain ranges such as the Hindu Kush between Pakistan and Afghanistan create natural obstacles.

★ ★ ☆

FORCE FACTS Some Special Forces units in Afghanistan rode horses—often sitting on highly uncomfortable wooden saddles— because of the primitive road system and mountainous terrain.

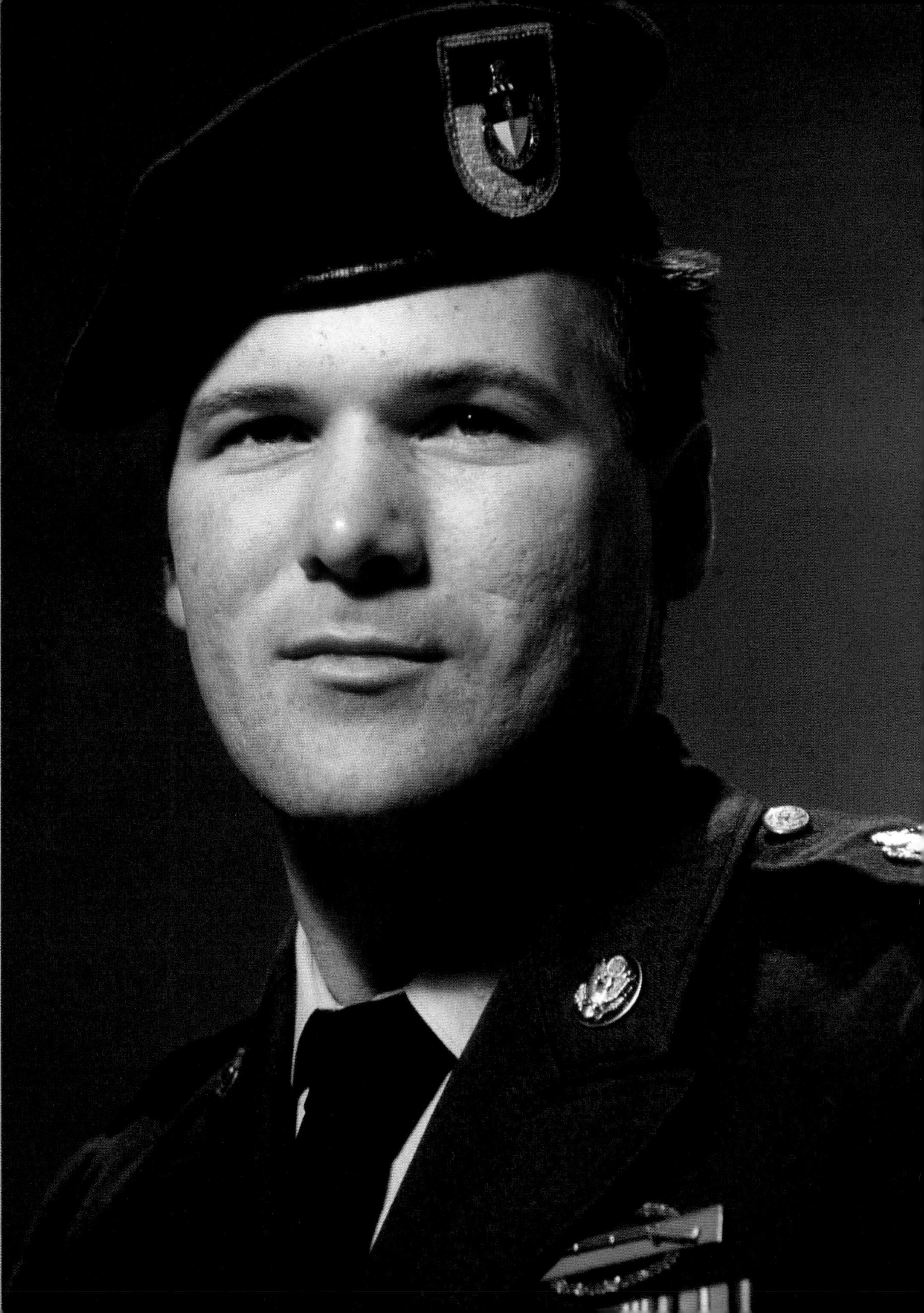

GREEN BERETS IN BOOKS AND MOVIES

U.S. SPECIAL FORCES

IT WOULD BE DIFFICULT TO FIND A MILITARY UNIT THAT HAS had as much media exposure—both favorable and otherwise—as the Green Berets. Many members of the regular army disapproved of the unit in the years immediately following its founding, but pressure from journalists in the early 1960s to satisfy the public's growing interest in these swashbuckling soldiers forced the army to provide access. Chief among these journalists was Robin Moore, a World War II airman who had been a Harvard University classmate of President Kennedy's brother Robert.

Moore drew on his friendship with Robert Kennedy to obtain unprecedented access to the Green Berets. This privilege came with a catch: the almost 40-year-old had to undergo actual Special Forces training. After several months, Moore was assigned to a Special Forces unit that was deployed to Vietnam in 1963. He drew upon his experiences to write a book called *The Green Berets*, which became a best seller when it was released (under the category of fiction) in 1965. "I decided I could present the truth better and more accurately in the form of fiction," Moore said. "I changed names and details, but I did not change the basic truth."

The following year, Moore collaborated with Sergeant Barry Sadler—a Special Forces soldier who had been wounded during his service in Vietnam—to produce the song "Ballad of the Green Berets." Like the book, the song portrayed Special Forces in a

Aspiring musician Barry Sadler was wounded by a punji stick, or booby-trapped stake.

positive light. It became a huge hit despite having to compete for airtime and purchase dollars with the likes of the Beatles and Rolling Stones. The song was dedicated to James Gabriel Jr., who had been captured and then executed by the Viet Cong in 1962 during a training mission. He was the first Special Forces soldier to die in the Vietnam War, and some of the song's lyrics refer specifically to him.

In the meantime, several attempts had been made to make a movie out of Moore's book. However, public opposition to the war had grown so strong that the army put many limitations on its cooperation with would-be filmmakers. Finally popular actor John Wayne—a supporter of the Vietnam War who was openly disgusted by its opponents—appealed directly to president Lyndon B. Johnson. "I told the president that I felt it was important that the people of the United States and also people all over the world should know why it was necessary for Americans to be in Vietnam," Wayne told his biographer Michael Munn. "And I got the government's support to make the picture." Even with the army's cooperation—allowing much of the filming to take place at Fort Benning in Georgia and supplying helicopters and other equipment, for instance—Wayne still encountered obstacles. He was finally able to produce the film, named *The Green Berets* and released in 1968, using his own money. Wayne starred as Colonel Mike Kirby, the leader of a Special Forces unit.

Much of the film revolves around journalist George Beckworth (played by David Janssen, best-known for his role in the TV series *The Fugitive*, which ran from 1963 to 1967). Beckworth is openly skeptical of U.S. involvement in Vietnam, but changes his mind after becoming *embedded* with Wayne's unit. One of the highlights of the film is a version of the attack on Nam Dong. At the end, a boy whom the Green Berets have befriended wonders what will happen to him. Col. Kirby puts a green beret on the boy's head and tells him, "You let me worry

Film critic Roger Ebert accused The Green Berets *of "depicting Vietnam in terms of cowboys and Indians."*

about that, Green Beret. You're what this thing's all about." Most film reviewers of the time gave the film low marks for glorifying the Vietnam War. Yet it was a commercial success. "The Duke [Wayne] always maintained that he was simply trying to remind the audience that soldiers were dying for them," said Scott McGee, a reviewer with the cable TV network Turner Classic Movies. "He knew about this firsthand because he had volunteered for a tour of Vietnam combat zones where he entertained troops, often at the risk of his own safety."

What neither Wayne nor the movie touched on, though, was the ongoing hostility that existed between the military establishment and Special Forces. This bad blood was attributed, in part, to the nature of Special Forces' covert actions. These were operations conducted outside the bounds of normal military procedure, which did not sit well with some in command. As former Special Forces officer Bob Seals notes, "Many generals could not hide their open disdain for Special Forces, with one Army Chief of Staff in the 1960s describing SF troops as 'refugees from responsibility' and that they 'tended to be nonconformists, couldn't quite get along in a straight military system.'"

Nevertheless, Seals continues, "The Military Assistance Advisory Command Intelligence Officer, or J-2, at one point during the war estimated that some 50 percent or so of all intelligence gathered daily was from SF and its sources. Some camps had such a level of knowledge that they were able to successfully identify Viet Cong, by name, operating in their area, and then quietly go about eliminating same." By war's end, Special Forces personnel would receive 17 Medals of Honor.

The tension came to a head in 1969, the year after *The Green Berets* was released. Colonel Robert Rheault, the newly appointed commanding officer of U.S. Special Forces in Vietnam, was court-martialed

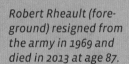

Robert Rheault (foreground) resigned from the army in 1969 and died in 2013 at age 87.

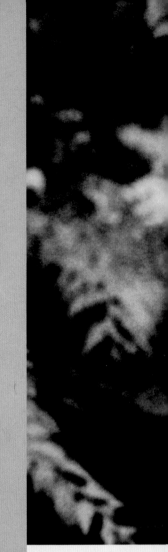

(along with six of his men) for allegedly executing a Vietnamese guide suspected of being a *double agent*. As the case drew national attention, many people believed that army leaders were trying to discredit Special Forces. The charges against Rheault eventually were dropped, but his career was ruined by what the press termed "the Green Beret case."

Rheault became the inspiration for the character of Special Forces Colonel Walter Kurtz (played by Marlon Brando) in the 1979 movie *Apocalypse Now*. Kurtz is accused of killing several suspected double agents. He retreats deep into the Cambodian jungle, where he establishes himself as head of an army consisting of hundreds of villagers reputed to be headhunters. Actor Martin Sheen plays Captain Benjamin Willard, a Special Forces officer who is ordered to track down Kurtz and kill him. The movie received numerous honors and today is widely regarded as one of the greatest anti-war films ever made.

In First Blood, *an ex-Green Beret's knowledge of guerrilla tactics makes him nearly impossible to stop.*

With the war in Vietnam winding down, Canadian novelist David Morrell addressed the problems American soldiers faced when they returned home in 1972's *First Blood*. The story's hero, John Rambo, served with distinction in Special Forces but suffers from psychological issues as a result. He begins a feud with a county sheriff—a former soldier who has a different set of values—that turns deadly as Rambo uses his Special Forces skills to evade capture and kill his pursuers. He, in turn, is hunted down and killed. In 1982, *First Blood* was adapted into a film starring Sylvester Stallone. Stallone rewrote the script, making Rambo a more sympathetic character and also keeping him alive at the end. *First Blood* was a huge hit with both moviegoers and critics, and, along with the *Rocky* series, made Stallone into one of Hollywood's biggest stars. The film also spawned three action-packed sequels that can be classified as war adventure thrillers set in foreign countries, and they do not have the same focus on Rambo's psychology.

Since the 1980s, Special Forces has remained visible in the media. Green Berets often play major roles in novels by bestselling authors such as Tom Clancy. The TV series *Person of Interest*, which began in 2011, features former Green Beret John Reese (played by Jim Caviezel) in a leading role. Reese's computer genius-partner predicts crimes that are about to occur, and Reese must prevent them by using his Special Forces skills. Jason Bourne, the central character in Robert Ludlum's popular Bourne Trilogy, learned his combat skills when he was a captain in the Green Berets. The series proved to be so popular that author Eric Van Lastbader has continued it for an additional seven installments. Even *The Simpsons* gets into the Special Forces act. Principal Skinner sometimes claims that he was a Green Beret in 'Nam. The audience chuckles, since his timid personality makes him the furthest thing from a genuine Green Beret.

Actor Matt Damon portrayed the conspiracy-obsessed Jason Bourne in 2002's The Bourne Identity *and two other films.*

FORCE FACTS One of the most famous lines from *Apocalypse Now*, "I love the smell of napalm [jellied gasoline] in the morning," is spoken by Robert Duvall's character as his helicopter gunships attack suspected enemy positions.

GREEN BERETS IN ACTION

DURING THE VIETNAM WAR, HUNDREDS OF AMERICAN pilots were shot down and held in prison camps in North Vietnam under conditions of near-barbarity. Aerial photographs revealed the location of one such camp in Son Tay, with a "K" scrawled in the dirt. The sign meant "Come get us," and Colonel Arthur "Bull" Simons was ready to answer the call.

Planning for a rescue mission began in May 1970. Training started in earnest three months later. Simons and a handpicked group of Green Berets rehearsed the dangerous operation over and over at a mockup of Son Tay at Florida's Eglin Air Force Base. Speed would be of the utmost importance. Thousands of North Vietnamese soldiers were stationed within a few miles of the camp. Simons knew that he and his men would have less than 30 minutes to carry out the mission before some of those enemy troops would begin to respond to the attack. During this brief window they not only had to overpower the guards but also carry dozens of weakened prisoners to the waiting helicopters.

Aided by an armada of more than 100 navy and air force aircraft, the raiders launched the assault shortly after 2:00 A.M. on November 21, 1970. The team split into four sections and searched the camp, killing dozens of guards without sustaining any *casualties*. But as the men dashed from building to building, they realized that there were no Americans. They learned later that the prisoners had been moved to another location several months earlier. Despite being unable to free the prisoners, and even though some of the attackers had landed in the wrong

When the North Vietnamese cut off a Green Beret camp in 1969, U.S. cargo planes dropped food and supplies.

GREEN BERETS rotated, 36.

FORCE FACTS The motto of Special Forces is the Latin phrase "De oppresso liber," which means "To free the oppressed."

location and had to fight their way out, the entire operation lasted just 27 minutes. Only two men received minor wounds. Today, the Son Tay raid is referred to as a "textbook" mission.

The ruins of the World Trade Center in New York City were still smoldering after the 9/11 attacks when president George W. Bush decided to attack Afghanistan. Controlled by the *Taliban*, the mountainous country had served as a training base for Osama bin Laden and the other terrorists who claimed responsibility for attacking the World Trade Center and the Pentagon. Because a full-scale invasion would take months to set up, Bush ordered Special Forces into the country immediately. One primary goal was to work with Afghan tribes and warlords who opposed the Taliban but didn't have the firepower or the training to oust them.

One of the first units to enter Afghanistan was A-574, commanded by Captain Jason Amerine. Accompanied by an Air Force Special Operations Command combat controller (CCT), the operators made contact with future Afghan leader Hamid Karzai and a few dozen of his followers on November 14, 2001. Karzai told the team that the nearby town of Tarin Kowt was the center of the Taliban movement. He recommended capturing it to deliver a huge psychological blow to the Taliban. Amerine had hoped to build a force of several hundred Afghans before making any attack. But before he could coordinate such an effort, the enthusiastic townspeople overthrew the Taliban administrators two days later.

Amerine decided to stay where he was and do the best he could with the forces he had on hand against the counterattack he knew would follow quickly, rather than waiting to recruit more fighters. As he explained, "The way a special forces team is set up, you're built to respond to things like this. I had my weapons sergeants analyzing the maps. I had my Air Force combat controller starting to figure out a plan to get a warning order

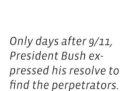

Only days after 9/11, President Bush expressed his resolve to find the perpetrators.

> **FORCE FACTS** The term guerrilla warfare—the specialty of Special Forces—is derived from a Spanish word that means "little wars."

kind of sent up to the Air Force and to the Navy that we'd probably need a lot of aircraft—fast. My communications sergeants were calling back right away to our higher headquarters, letting them know what was coming our way. JD, the team sergeant, was there orchestrating everything, making sure that everybody was kind of staying on task."

Amerine set up his defenses south of town. The Taliban quickly regrouped and sent a force of upwards of 500 men to retake the town. They carried heavy machine guns that were more powerful than anything that A-574 and the Afghans had. As the CCT began calling in air strikes, many of Karzai's men—who had never seen such destructive power—fled in panic.

Amerine ordered a retreat back to town. He urged Karzai to order his men back into place. "All the aircraft in the world weren't going to help us once the Taliban got into the town and it turned into a military operation on urban terrain, because we couldn't exactly bomb the town to save it," Amerine explained later. "So if we couldn't stop them before they got into the town, the fight was lost." Although the Taliban now occupied Amerine's original positions, the Americans and Afghans had the advantage of continual air strikes. Several hours later, the Taliban were gone for good, leaving behind hundreds of casualties. That cleared the way for an advance to be made on Kandahar, the final remaining Taliban stronghold, which surrendered on December 5. The operation to overthrow the Taliban—which many experts had estimated could take several months—was over in a matter of weeks.

Less than two years later, the U.S. launched Operation Iraqi Freedom to overthrow the country's longtime dictator Saddam Hussein. On April 6, 2003, two and a half weeks after the start of the conflict, a small group of Green

Hamid Karzai became the first democratically elected president of Afghanistan in 2004.

Berets was detailed to a crucial road junction near the village of Debecka. The junction lay between the cities of Kirkuk and Mosul in the northern part of the country and its capture would seriously impede the movement of Iraqi forces.

The Green Berets, aided by local Kurdish fighters, easily accomplished their objective, and then moved forward to get closer to the flow of Iraqi army traffic. A thick haze covered the area. Soon, three trucks emerged, blinking their headlights. These were followed by six armored personnel carriers and four battle tanks. All in all, several hundred Iraqis were now bearing down on the unit.

The Americans and Kurds scrambled up a nearby ridge. Halfway up, they found a slight depression that allowed them to take shelter. "We all made a mental promise," said Staff Sergeant Jeffrey Adamec. "Nobody had to yell out commands. Everybody just knew. We were not going to move back from that point. We were not going to give up that ground. We called that

In 2005, Green Berets fought alongside Iraqi forces to battle insurgent, or rebel, snipers.

spot 'the Alamo.'" Unlike its namesake, this "Alamo" turned out to be successfully defendable.

Adamec and Staff Sergeant Jason Brown fired Javelin missiles at the attackers, scoring several direct hits. "Two guys shut down the attack," said their battalion commanding officer, Major Curtis W. Hubbard. "Two guys turned an organized Iraqi attack into chaos. They halted an entire motorized rifle company."

The CCTs called in air support, which completed the work of the two sergeants in halting the assault. Soon afterward, a number of Iraqis left their positions and waved pieces of white paper. Two white SUVs drove up to them. Several men in flowing white robes emerged and executed the hapless soldiers. The Americans were furious. "We called in an F-18 to drop a 750-pound bomb on those SUVs," said Captain Eric Wright, who commanded one of the Green Beret units. "It was like a magic show. You know, now you see 'em, now you don't. The SUVs, the guys in the white robes—they simply vanished." So did the Iraqi attack. Without losing a single man, the Green Berets destroyed nearly two dozen vehicles and killed scores of enemy soldiers.

Son Tay, Tarin Kowt, and Debecka are just three of hundreds of engagements in which Green Berets have distinguished themselves. No longer considered empty threats or distasteful nonconformists, Green Berets are among the most highly trained and dedicated warriors in the entire American military. From the jungles of Vietnam to the remote mountains of Afghanistan, they've proven that they are especially dangerous to this country's enemies.

Special forces use a technique called helo-casting to drop from a helicopter into water.

FORCE FACTS Some missions require landing on coastlines, so the men learn how to paddle lightweight rubber boats and even kayaks.

In high altitude–low opening (HALO) jumping, parachutists free-fall for a period of time.

FORCE FACTS Special Forces utilizes high-altitude parachute jumping because no one on the ground is able to hear the sound of the engines of the approaching aircraft.

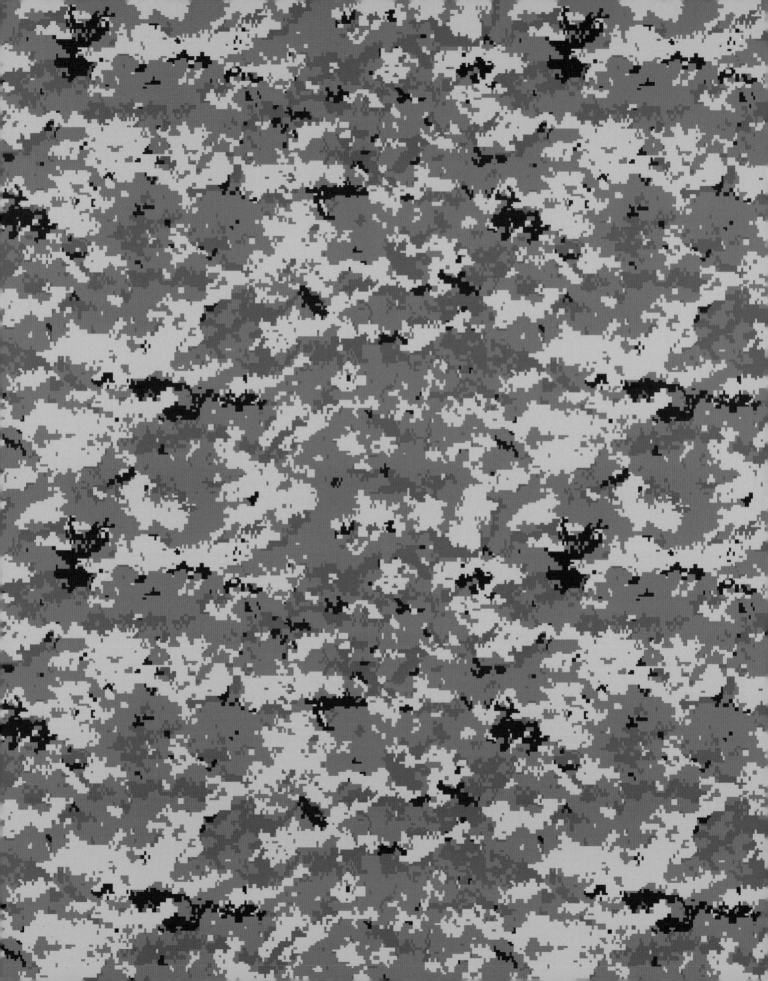

GLOSSARY

attrition – the process of gradually reducing the size and strength of a military unit as a result of personnel departures

casualties – people injured or killed in an accident or a battle

coup – a sudden, illegal seizure of a government, often by violent means

double agent – someone who acts as a spy for one country while pretending to spy for another

embedded – attached to a military unit

enlisted men – those who sign up voluntarily for military duty at a rank below an officer; they compose the largest part of military units

exfiltration – removal of personnel from enemy-controlled territory

fast-roping – sliding down a thick rope suspended from a helicopter as rapidly as possible

French and Indian War – a conflict (1754–63) between France and Great Britain for control of North America

guerrilla – a fighter who isn't part of conventional armed forces

indigenous – originating or living in a particular location

infiltration – secretive passage into enemy-held territory

insurgency – an unorganized rebellion against a government

rappelling – descending a vertical surface using a rope coiled around the body and attached at a higher point

shrapnel – sharp fragments from an exploding bomb or bullet

squad automatic weapon – a lightweight machine gun offering a portable source of automatic weaponry to a small unit

Taliban – a fundamentalist Islamic political movement and militia that controlled Afghanistan; noted especially for terror tactics and a repressive attitude toward women

unconventional warfare – warfare conducted behind enemy lines, usually by small groups of fighters

warrant officer – a military officer ranking above a noncommissioned officer and below a commissioned officer

FORCE FACTS The Special Forces patch is in the shape of an arrowhead. It contains a vertical sword crossed by three lightning bolts, and the word "Airborne" is on top.

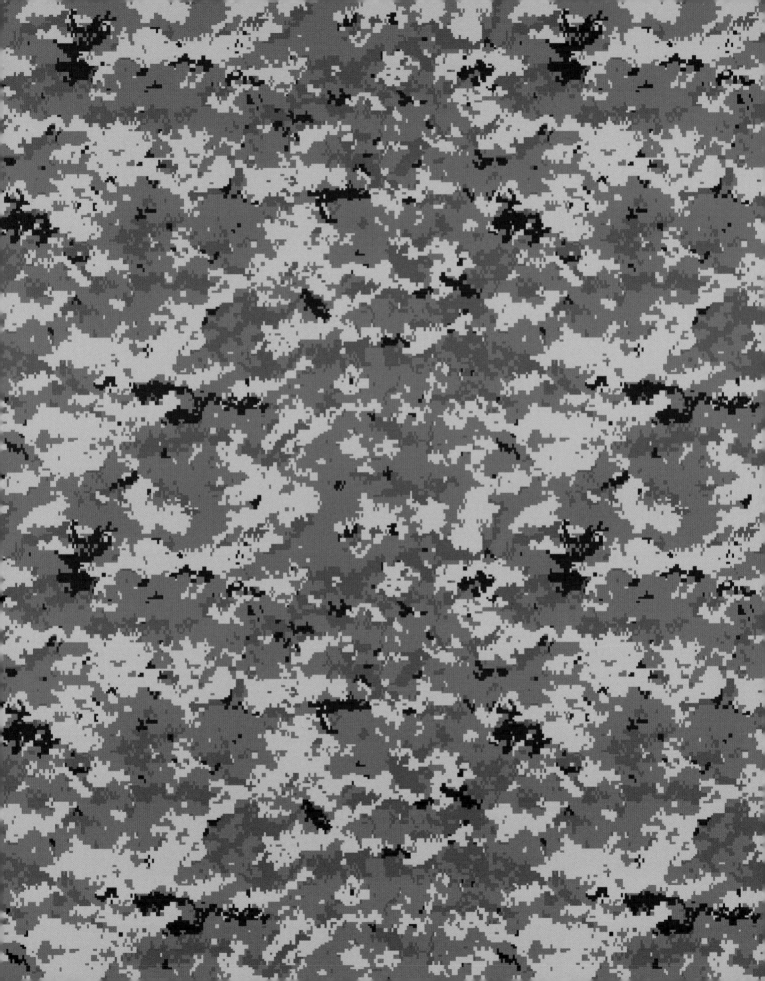

SELECTED BIBLIOGRAPHY

Cantrell, Mark, and Donald Vaughan. *Special Forces: America's Elite*. Bonita Springs, Fla.: The Media Source, 2012.

Clancy, Tom, and John Gresham. *Special Forces: A Guided Tour of U.S. Army Special Forces*. New York: Berkley Books, 2001.

Couch, Dick. *Chosen Soldier: The Making of a Special Forces Warrior*. New York: Crown, 2007.

Frederick, Jim. *Special Ops: The Hidden World of America's Toughest Warriors*. New York: Time Books, 2011.

Halberstadt, Hans. *War Stories of the Green Berets*. St. Paul, Minn.: Zenith Press, 2004.

Moore, Robin. *The Green Berets: The Amazing Story of the U.S. Army's Elite Special Forces Unit*. New York: Skyhorse Publishing, 2007.

North, Oliver. *American Heroes in Special Operations*. Nashville: Fidelis Books, 2010.

Zimmerman, Dwight Jon, and John D. Gresham. *Beyond Hell and Back: How America's Special Operations Forces Became the World's Greatest Fighting Unit*. New York: St. Martin's Press, 2007.

WEBSITES

Interview with U.S. Army Captain Jason Amerine

http://www.pbs.org/wgbh/pages/frontline/shows /campaign/interviews/amerine.html

A Public Broadcasting System transcript of an interview with Captain Amerine offers an in-depth account of the Battle of Tarin Kowt.

Special Forces – GoArmy.com

http://www.goarmy.com/special-forces.html

The official U.S. Army website has information on qualifications, benefits, training methods, A-team job descriptions, and more.

READ MORE

Brush, Jim. *Special Forces*. Mankato, Minn.: Sea-to-Sea, 2012.

Cooper, Jason. *U.S. Special Operations*. Vero Beach, Fla.: Rourke, 2004.

INDEX

U.S. SPECIAL FORCES